JOY Journal

RCI Publishing & RCI Institute

ISBN: 978-1-7923-5329-1

Printed in the United States of America.

JOY *Journal*

5 Minutes a Day to More
Motivation, Clarity and Joy

A SELF-GUIDED
daily journal

JOURNAL

Belongs to:

____

create your journey...

Taking a moment to breathe and reflect allows you to turn on your personal power giving you clarity, acceptance, and inner strength. Self-reflection helps you focus on what matters most in your life and allows you to shift out of your HeadTrash, (those little people in your brain that talk trash, suck your energy, increase your stress and keep you in worry and fear); and move you into positivity, motivation and inner strength.

Understanding the Why About HeadTrash & Joy

As explored in my book, **HEADTRASH: *The Leading Killer of Human Potential***, I delve deep into the critical role that emotions play in creating the life you want and most importantly finding more joy in your journey.

We all have what I call "an emotional brain". Your emotional brain runs your life. The key to unlocking motivation and unleashing your potential lies in living in the connected side of your emotional brain. This is where your personal power comes to life, enabling you to decrease stress, gain clarity, solve problems effectively, and turn up your motivation.

We all know that having a positive mind set matters and yet sometimes it is just hard to find when our lives are throwing us into endless chaos and negativity is hitting us from all angles. This negativity lives in the disconnected side of your emotional brain. In this domain, fear, worry, mistakes, problems, and unproductive actions take root, sucking your energy, joy and potential.

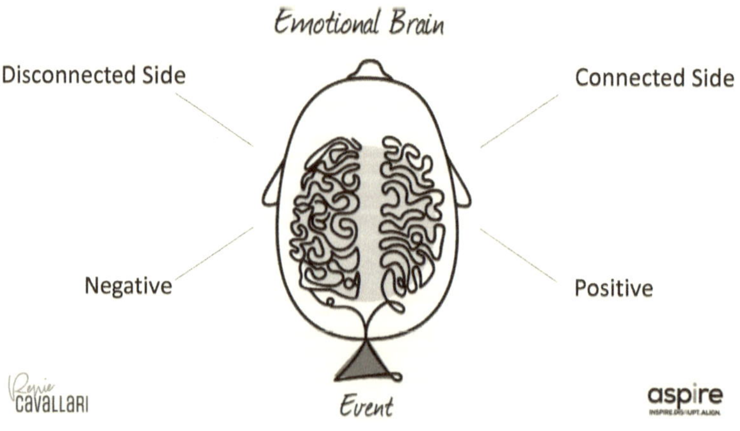

What's the point?

Based on working hands-on with thousands of people from around the globe, mindset is the most important predictor of how we experience life **and** HeadTrash is the active ingredient when our mind set is negative and undermining us. This research found a clear correlation between how we think and how happy we are.

The more you think you can't do something, the more your behavior will reflect those thoughts and the worse you will feel. Your thoughts determine your focus, and your focus determines your actions. Your actions determine your results from productivity to joy.

The facts about the Disconnected Side of Your Emotional Brain

The disconnected side is driven by a variety of negative energy producers like fear, anxiety, and worry. Operating your life from the disconnected side is like living life with the lights turned off. The dark is anxiety provoking, unclear and easily overwhelming.

You want to live in the connected side of your emotional brain where positivity, motivation, solutions and happiness live. When you live in the connected side you will decrease your stress, gain clarity and take productive action which is at the heart of getting out of the feeling of "being stuck" or hopeless.

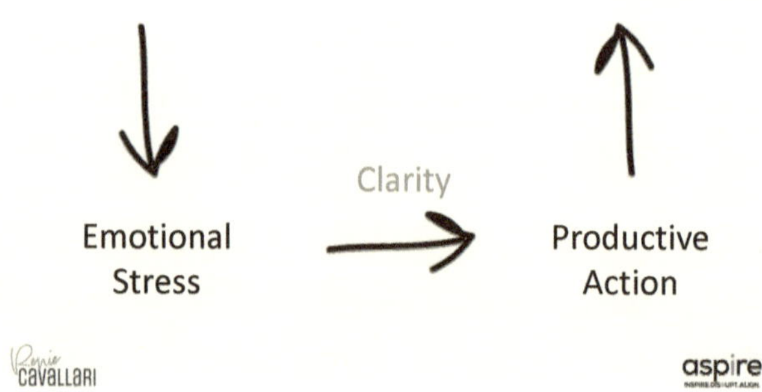

One of the most important ways to turn on your motivational switch and joy meter is to start your day on the connected side. If you begin your day with the negativity of the news, or the time sucking nature of social media, or just being rushed each morning, you will increase your emotional stress, and this creates chaos. Chaos sucks our energy and disrupts our focus.

We can't control the world. We can't control other people. We can't control many aspects of our day or work. What we can control is how we think, and the quality of our lives reflects how much time we live in the connected side of our emotional brain. This we can control when we learn how to manage, and ideally dump our HeadTrash and set our focus in the direction of what matters most each day.

If you start your day in chaos, odds are you will spend your day the same way.

The point of the Joy Journal is to help you start your day on the connected side of your emotional brain where your best self and life lives.

What Will The Joy Journal Do for You?

1. **Boost Motivation & Positivity:** Begin each day with a powerful dose of positivity, clarity, and courage. It's your daily ritual to set the tone for your own greatness.

2. **Eliminate Life's Hurdles:** Watch as life's upsets and challenges lose their

grip on you. By shifting your focus and harnessing your personal power, you'll find yourself overcoming obstacles with grace.

3. **Conquer Your HeadTrash:** Bid farewell to the negative self-talk that often holds you back. Embrace a more productive and positive perspective that empowers you to take on the world.

How Often Should I Journal?

Just 5-10 minutes each morning. Think of it this way. You brush your teeth and shower to keep your body clean and healthy. Take the time to journal to keep your mind clear and inspired.

In exchange for 5-10 minutes of your day, you will find more joy in your life… it's a pretty good exchange rate.

What Happens if I Miss a Day?

There are no dates in the journal, so no guilt is required to participate! (Guilt lives in the disconnected side and steals your peace of mind!). You will date the page and journal for that day. Missed a day? Get back to it tomorrow.

Journaling Made Simple

I created this journal approach for me. I may be a writer, but I am not a journaler! I have a crazy busy life and I needed something to help me start my day off optimally with positivity, clarity and, on the connected side of my emotional brain. Here is what I suggest:

Step 1: Find a quiet place. Sometimes my house is so crazy, that my quiet place is in the bathroom!

Step 2: Close your eyes. Breathe in, hold it and breath out. Repeat. Breathing deeply helps us move to the connected side and literally lowers our raising heart rate.

Step 3: Reflect on and answer each question. These questions ensure you are starting your day in your power, the connected side. The questions you ask yourself determine your thoughts and you feel the way you think. These specific questions will help you decrease your emotional stress, gain clarity and therefore ensure you are motivated and focused on productive action for the day.

I have personally used these questions for decades to help me live on the connected side, stay out of my HeadTrash and my world of self-created chaos and find more joy in my daily journey.

1. **What is my word of the day?** Your word of the day sets your intention and allows you to check in on that intention throughout the day. Examples include: Focus. Productive. Fun. Appreciation. Creativity. Strategic. Inspiring. Kindness. Grateful. Curious. Disciplined. Process-focused. Engaging. Listen. And my favorite, Love.

2. **What HeadTrash do I need to dump from yesterday?** Owning your HeadTrash and disappointments helps you let go of that negative self-talk and move to the connected side of your emotional brain. There is something about writing down your trash that helps you start to dump it. Write away!

3. **What went well yesterday?** This question helps you shift out of your HeadTrash and allows you to focus on productivity. There is nothing like productivity to make us feel like we are making progress, (no matter how small) and this stirs momentum. Now you are not stuck, you are motivated.

4. **What is important for me to focus on and accomplish today?** Clarity gives you focus, and this allows you to take productive action. Productive action creates progress and feelings of self-worth.

5. **At this moment, what am I grateful for?** Gratitude puts you in the connected side of your emotional brain and in the ideal mindset. It reminds you of what you have and embraces feelings of appreciation vs. expectation or disappointment. Gratitude is your secret fuel injector as it fuels your positive energy.

In a world that sometimes rushes us along and frequently throws us into the disconnected side of our emotional brain, this journal is meant to encourage you to pause, reflect, and shift your life into what matters most, **how much joy is in your life.**

I hope this journal is your guide to living life with greater purpose, positivity, and fulfillment—one journal entry at a time.

Live in Joy!

-Renie

Shine Your Light

_____ / _____ / 20_____

What is my word of the day? _______________________________

What HeadTrash do I need to dump from yesterday?

What went well yesterday?

What is important for me to focus on and accomplish today?

At this moment, what am I grateful for?

What I focus on comes true.

_______ / _______ / 20_______

What is my word of the day? ____

What HeadTrash do I need to dump from yesterday?

____

____

____

What went well yesterday?

____

____

____

What is important for me to focus on and accomplish today?

____

____

____

At this moment, what am I grateful for?

____

____

____

The difference between the possible and the impossible is in my determination.

Shine Your Light

_____ / _____ / 20_____

What is my word of the day? _______________________________

What HeadTrash do I need to dump from yesterday?

____

____

____

What went well yesterday?

____

____

____

What is important for me to focus on and accomplish today?

____

____

____

At this moment, what am I grateful for?

____

____

____

What if I knew I could do anything? Then, what would I do?

#DUMPHeadTrash

____ / ____ / 20____

What is my word of the day? ____

What HeadTrash do I need to dump from yesterday?

What went well yesterday?

What is important for me to focus on and accomplish today?

At this moment, what am I grateful for?

It is in my deepest moments of frustration that I know I am in the depths of learning.

Shine Your Light

_____ / _____ / 20_____

What is my word of the day? ____

What HeadTrash do I need to dump from yesterday?

What went well yesterday?

What is important for me to focus on and accomplish today?

At this moment, what am I grateful for?

What would I do if I knew I could not fail?

#DUMPHeadTrash

_____ / _____ / 20 _____

What is my word of the day? ______________________________________

What HeadTrash do I need to dump from yesterday?

What went well yesterday?

What is important for me to focus on and accomplish today?

At this moment, what am I grateful for?

The only thing in my way is me.

Shine Your Light

_____ / _____ / 20_____

What is my word of the day? _______________________________________

What HeadTrash do I need to dump from yesterday?

What went well yesterday?

What is important for me to focus on and accomplish today?

At this moment, what am I grateful for?

Passion is the fuel of life. It is my sword.

_____ / _____ / 20_____

What is my word of the day? _______________________________________

What HeadTrash do I need to dump from yesterday?

What went well yesterday?

What is important for me to focus on and accomplish today?

At this moment, what am I grateful for?

Everything I need is within me right now.

THE LABYRINTH

a poem by Renie

Life is a journey.
Like the labyrinth,
its beauty resides in its twists and turns.
Self-reflection exposes my self-deception.
Acceptance and appreciation replace
disappointment and expectation.

My life's purpose is at the
center of my labyrinth.
It's my journey's compass.
The journey is how I live and how I love.
How I give and receive.
How I touch the lives of others.
How I chose to create my world.

Like the labyrinth,
I sometimes feel like I am going in circles.
I breathe into the rhythm of each step.
I embrace the silence and hold onto my faith.
Silence will bring me the clarity I long for.

And then the haze lifts.
I see my path again.
With each passing chapter,
my life's labyrinth continues to expand.
My light shines brightly so I can see.
There in the center of it all, I find my true self.
The self I am meant to be.

#DUMPHeadTrash

_____ / _____ / 20_____

What is my word of the day? ____

What HeadTrash do I need to dump from yesterday?

What went well yesterday?

What is important for me to focus on and accomplish today?

At this moment, what am I grateful for?

What am I willing to do to have what I want?

Shine Your Light

_____ / _____ / 20 _____

What is my word of the day? ____

What HeadTrash do I need to dump from yesterday?

____

____

____

What went well yesterday?

____

____

____

What is important for me to focus on and accomplish today?

____

____

____

At this moment, what am I grateful for?

____

____

____

Fear, like guilt, is an illusion we create.

#DUMPHeadTrash

_____ / _____ / 20_____

What is my word of the day? _______________________________________

What HeadTrash do I need to dump from yesterday?

What went well yesterday?

What is important for me to focus on and accomplish today?

At this moment, what am I grateful for?

Pessimism is the poison of all that is possible.

Shine Your Light

_____ / _____ / 20_____

What is my word of the day? ____

What HeadTrash do I need to dump from yesterday?

What went well yesterday?

What is important for me to focus on and accomplish today?

At this moment, what am I grateful for?

The only limits I have are in my head.

#DUMPHeadTrash

_____ / _____ / 20_____

What is my word of the day? _______________________________________

What HeadTrash do I need to dump from yesterday?

____

____

____

What went well yesterday?

____

____

____

What is important for me to focus on and accomplish today?

____

____

____

At this moment, what am I grateful for?

____

____

____

There is no future living in my past.

Shine Your Light

_____ / _____ / 20_____

What is my word of the day? ____

What HeadTrash do I need to dump from yesterday?

____

____

____

What went well yesterday?

____

____

____

What is important for me to focus on and accomplish today?

____

____

____

At this moment, what am I grateful for?

____

____

____

I trust that everything works out in my favor.

#DUMPHeadTrash

_____ / _____ / 20_____

What is my word of the day? ____

What HeadTrash do I need to dump from yesterday?

What went well yesterday?

What is important for me to focus on and accomplish today?

At this moment, what am I grateful for?

If I want extraordinary results, I have to do extraordinary things.

Shine Your Light

______ / ______ / 20______

What is my word of the day? ____

What HeadTrash do I need to dump from yesterday?

What went well yesterday?

What is important for me to focus on and accomplish today?

At this moment, what am I grateful for?

I have all the time there is.

JOY

a poem by Renie

Joy… a space within me that is quiet,
still, and at peace.

A feeling of happiness and gratitude.

A sense of being grounded in purpose.

A place of appreciation.

I create it.
I give it.
I live within it.

Joy… is the true measure of success.

Shine Your Light

____ / ____ / 20____

What is my word of the day? _______________________________

What HeadTrash do I need to dump from yesterday?

What went well yesterday?

What is important for me to focus on and accomplish today?

At this moment, what am I grateful for?

I am blessed and divinely guided.

#DUMPHeadTrash

_____ / _____ / 20_____

What is my word of the day? ______________________________

What HeadTrash do I need to dump from yesterday?

What went well yesterday?

What is important for me to focus on and accomplish today?

At this moment, what am I grateful for?

I can change anything if I change how I think.

Shine Your Light

_____ / _____ / 20 _____

What is my word of the day? ____

What HeadTrash do I need to dump from yesterday?

What went well yesterday?

What is important for me to focus on and accomplish today?

At this moment, what am I grateful for?

How I play is how I live.

____ / ____ / 20____

What is my word of the day? ____

What HeadTrash do I need to dump from yesterday?

What went well yesterday?

What is important for me to focus on and accomplish today?

At this moment, what am I grateful for?

Stop trying to fit in...you were born to stand out.

Shine Your Light

____ / ____ / 20____

What is my word of the day? _______________________________

What HeadTrash do I need to dump from yesterday?

What went well yesterday?

What is important for me to focus on and accomplish today?

At this moment, what am I grateful for?

Forgiveness sets me free.

What is my word of the day? ____

What HeadTrash do I need to dump from yesterday?

____

____

____

What went well yesterday?

____

____

____

What is important for me to focus on and accomplish today?

____

____

____

At this moment, what am I grateful for?

____

____

____

Shine Your Light

_____ / _____ / 20_____

What is my word of the day? ____

What HeadTrash do I need to dump from yesterday?

____

____

____

What went well yesterday?

____

____

____

What is important for me to focus on and accomplish today?

____

____

____

At this moment, what am I grateful for?

____

____

____

I am who I choose to be, and, in those choices, I live.

#DUMPHeadTrash

_____ / _____ / 20_____

What is my word of the day? ______________________________

What HeadTrash do I need to dump from yesterday?

____

____

____

What went well yesterday?

____

____

What is important for me to focus on and accomplish today?

____

____

____

At this moment, what am I grateful for?

____

____

____

Choose to be happy.

SHINE YOUR LIGHT
a poem by Renie

I shine when I live my life
in gratitude.

I shine when I give compassion
to others.

I shine when I give my best self.

I shine when my smile
brightens someone's day.

I shine when I take productive
action against life's challenges.

I shine when I sprinkle kindness.

I shine when I play all in.

I shine my light, and in doing so,
I light the way for others to see what might be
possible.

I am a Shiner.

_____ / _____ / 20_____

What is my word of the day? _______________________________________

What HeadTrash do I need to dump from yesterday?

What went well yesterday?

What is important for me to focus on and accomplish today?

At this moment, what am I grateful for?

Set your spirit free.

Shine Your Light

_____ / _____ / 20_____

What is my word of the day? ____

What HeadTrash do I need to dump from yesterday?

____

____

____

What went well yesterday?

____

____

____

What is important for me to focus on and accomplish today?

____

____

____

At this moment, what am I grateful for?

____

____

____

I am soley responsible for my life.

_____ / _____ / 20_____

What is my word of the day? ____

What HeadTrash do I need to dump from yesterday?

____

____

____

What went well yesterday?

____

____

____

What is important for me to focus on and accomplish today?

____

____

____

At this moment, what am I grateful for?

____

____

____

Small minds...small talk. Open minds...unlimited potential.

Shine Your Light

_____ / _____ / 20_____

What is my word of the day? _______________________________________

What HeadTrash do I need to dump from yesterday?

What went well yesterday?

What is important for me to focus on and accomplish today?

At this moment, what am I grateful for?

Learning is the gift I give my soul.

#DUMPHeadTrash

_____ / _____ / 20_____

What is my word of the day? ____

What HeadTrash do I need to dump from yesterday?

What went well yesterday?

What is important for me to focus on and accomplish today?

At this moment, what am I grateful for?

How I see the world is how I experience my life.

Shine Your Light

_____ / _____ / 20 _____

What is my word of the day? _______________________________________

What HeadTrash do I need to dump from yesterday?

____

____

____

What went well yesterday?

____

____

____

What is important for me to focus on and accomplish today?

____

____

____

At this moment, what am I grateful for?

____

____

____

When I let go of anger and judgement towards others, I find inner peace.

#DUMPHeadTrash

_______ / _______ / 20_______

What is my word of the day? ____

What HeadTrash do I need to dump from yesterday?

____

____

____

What went well yesterday?

____

____

____

What is important for me to focus on and accomplish today?

____

____

____

At this moment, what am I grateful for?

____

____

____

Find joy in the little things.

Shine Your Light

____ / ____ / 20____

What is my word of the day? ____

What HeadTrash do I need to dump from yesterday?

What went well yesterday?

What is important for me to focus on and accomplish today?

At this moment, what am I grateful for?

I can change anything when I choose to.

LOVE

a poem by Renie

Love is a gift in our lives.
It enriches our world and feeds our soul.
Love can help us soar to our greatest heights and can take us
to our knees.

Love clarifies what matters
most in our lives.
It requires us to balance our needs
with the needs of the people we love.
To feel the soft embrace that love provides, requires us to not
just give love,
but to also receive it.

It is the love of oneself that gives us strength as we navigate
the challenges of life's journey.
It is this self-love that allows us to love and accept another
without fear of rejection.

To love deeply is to jump. To risk.
To not allow the inevitable disappointments to deter us from
the joy that only love brings.

We have been given an endless supply of love.
It is through love that we find what is best in ourselves,
in others, and in our lives.

Love is all there is.

Shine Your Light

____ / ____ / 20____

What is my word of the day? ____

What HeadTrash do I need to dump from yesterday?

What went well yesterday?

What is important for me to focus on and accomplish today?

At this moment, what am I grateful for?

The only limits in my life are the limits I create.

____ / ____ / 20____

What is my word of the day? ____

What HeadTrash do I need to dump from yesterday?

What went well yesterday?

What is important for me to focus on and accomplish today?

At this moment, what am I grateful for?

I relinquish control and allow others to support me.

Shine Your Light

____ / ____ / 20____

What is my word of the day? ___________________________

What HeadTrash do I need to dump from yesterday?

What went well yesterday?

What is important for me to focus on and accomplish today?

At this moment, what am I grateful for?

Who I spend time with is who I become.

#DUMPHeadTrash

_____ / _____ / 20 _____

What is my word of the day? _______________________________

What HeadTrash do I need to dump from yesterday?

____

____

____

What went well yesterday?

____

____

____

What is important for me to focus on and accomplish today?

____

____

____

At this moment, what am I grateful for?

____

____

____

Nothing kills progress like the need for perfection.

Shine Your Light

_____ / _____ / 20_____

What is my word of the day? ____

What HeadTrash do I need to dump from yesterday?

What went well yesterday?

What is important for me to focus on and accomplish today?

At this moment, what am I grateful for?

Nothing positive comes from negativity.

#DUMPHeadTrash

_____ / _____ / 20_____

What is my word of the day? ____

What HeadTrash do I need to dump from yesterday?

What went well yesterday?

What is important for me to focus on and accomplish today?

At this moment, what am I grateful for?

Today I choose to live to my true potential

Shine Your Light

____ / ____ / 20____

What is my word of the day? ______________________________

What HeadTrash do I need to dump from yesterday?

What went well yesterday?

What is important for me to focus on and accomplish today?

At this moment, what am I grateful for?

Creating momentum in a new direction is the first step to effecting change.

#DUMPHeadTrash

_____ / _____ / 20_____

What is my word of the day? ____

What HeadTrash do I need to dump from yesterday?

What went well yesterday?

What is important for me to focus on and accomplish today?

At this moment, what am I grateful for?

If I don't like what I see around me, it's time to stop and reflect.

GRATEFUL

a poem by Renie

Be grateful for the lovers
and the haters.
The courageous and the passionate.
The pukers and the raving fans.

Be grateful for the shine the lighters.
And the up all-nighters.
For the inspiration and the perspiration.
The hard work, the dedication,
and the endless collaboration.
The joyful, the humble, and the real.

Be grateful for the journey.
For the bumps in the road and
those perfect road trip days.
For those that challenge you
and for those that challenge the status quo.
For the extraordinary people
you get to hang with
and all the lessons learned along the way.

Be grateful for those who raise your bar
and those who trust you to raise theirs.
For those that bring you joy
and those that help you
find light in the darkness.

These are your people.
The believers. The teachers.
The cheerleaders.

Be grateful and LIVE ALL IN!

#DUMPHeadTrash

______ / ______ / 20______

What is my word of the day? ____

What HeadTrash do I need to dump from yesterday?

What went well yesterday?

What is important for me to focus on and accomplish today?

At this moment, what am I grateful for?

Today, I will check in on my thoughts. Are they serving me or limiting me?

Shine Your Light

_____ / _____ / 20_____

What is my word of the day? ____

What HeadTrash do I need to dump from yesterday?

____

____

____

What went well yesterday?

____

____

____

What is important for me to focus on and accomplish today?

____

____

____

At this moment, what am I grateful for?

____

____

____

What matters most, is what I'm doing first!

#DUMPHeadTrash

____ / ____ / 20____

What is my word of the day? ____

What HeadTrash do I need to dump from yesterday?

What went well yesterday?

What is important for me to focus on and accomplish today?

At this moment, what am I grateful for?

I am the captain of my life.

Shine Your Light

_____ / _____ / 20_____

What is my word of the day? ____

What HeadTrash do I need to dump from yesterday?

What went well yesterday?

What is important for me to focus on and accomplish today?

At this moment, what am I grateful for?

Growth awakens my potential.

#DUMPHeadTrash

_____ / _____ / 20_____

What is my word of the day? ____

What HeadTrash do I need to dump from yesterday?

____

____

____

What went well yesterday?

____

____

____

What is important for me to focus on and accomplish today?

____

____

____

At this moment, what am I grateful for?

____

____

____

I choose to see what is right and move forward.

Shine Your Light

_____ / _____ / 20 _____

What is my word of the day? _______________________________________

What HeadTrash do I need to dump from yesterday?

What went well yesterday?

What is important for me to focus on and accomplish today?

At this moment, what am I grateful for?

A small step in a new direction is always better than a grand idea standing still.

#DUMPHeadTrash

_____ / _____ / 20_____

What is my word of the day? ____

What HeadTrash do I need to dump from yesterday?

What went well yesterday?

What is important for me to focus on and accomplish today?

At this moment, what am I grateful for?

Success is a result of thoughtFULL action.

Shine Your Light

_____ / _____ / 20_____

What is my word of the day? ____

What HeadTrash do I need to dump from yesterday?

____

____

____

What went well yesterday?

____

____

____

What is important for me to focus on and accomplish today?

____

____

____

At this moment, what am I grateful for?

____

____

____

I am the only person who controls my mindset.

BE WHO YOU ARE

a poem by Renie

Be who you are.

Not an imitation of someone else.

Not someone you think you are
supposed to be.

Not your work or the car you drive.

You are the choices you make.

The actions you take.

The positive impact you create.

Who you are is who you choose to be.

Shine Your Light

_____ / _____ / 20_____

What is my word of the day? _______________________________

What HeadTrash do I need to dump from yesterday?

____

____

____

What went well yesterday?

____

____

____

What is important for me to focus on and accomplish today?

____

____

____

At this moment, what am I grateful for?

____

____

____

Who I hang with is who I become.

#DUMPHeadTrash

_____ / _____ / 20_____

What is my word of the day? ____

What HeadTrash do I need to dump from yesterday?

What went well yesterday?

What is important for me to focus on and accomplish today?

At this moment, what am I grateful for?

If it's to be, it's up to me!

Shine Your Light

_____ / _____ / 20_____

What is my word of the day? _______________________________________

What HeadTrash do I need to dump from yesterday?

What went well yesterday?

What is important for me to focus on and accomplish today?

At this moment, what am I grateful for?

My thoughts determine my actions. My actions reflect my life.

What is my word of the day? ____

What HeadTrash do I need to dump from yesterday?

What went well yesterday?

What is important for me to focus on and accomplish today?

At this moment, what am I grateful for?

NOW is the right time to move towards what I want in my life.

Shine Your Light

_____ / _____ / 20_____

What is my word of the day? ____

What HeadTrash do I need to dump from yesterday?

What went well yesterday?

What is important for me to focus on and accomplish today?

At this moment, what am I grateful for?

Mistakes happen!

_____ / _____ / 20_____

What is my word of the day? ________________________________

What HeadTrash do I need to dump from yesterday?

____

____

____

What went well yesterday?

____

____

____

What is important for me to focus on and accomplish today?

____

____

____

At this moment, what am I grateful for?

____

____

____

Change is inevitable. Growth is optional.

Shine Your Light

_____ / _____ / 20_____

What is my word of the day? ____

What HeadTrash do I need to dump from yesterday?

What went well yesterday?

What is important for me to focus on and accomplish today?

At this moment, what am I grateful for?

I have the right to be happy, successful, and in love.

What is my word of the day? _______________________________

What HeadTrash do I need to dump from yesterday?

What went well yesterday?

What is important for me to focus on and accomplish today?

At this moment, what am I grateful for?

I can't have it if I don't feel it.

THE COURAGE WITHIN

a poem by Renie

Finding the courage to preserver
can be the toughest part
of life's journey.

It requires us to show up when
others may choose not to.
To find laughter in times of worry.
To find light in the darkness.

Courage requires inner strength so
we can consider another perspective
when ours is the only one we want to hear.
It helps us engage
when apathy is creeping in.
And, allows us let go
when control is what feels safest.

Courage is life's parachute.

Never be afraid to put the cord.

_____ / _____ / 20_____

What is my word of the day? _______________________________

What HeadTrash do I need to dump from yesterday?

What went well yesterday?

What is important for me to focus on and accomplish today?

At this moment, what am I grateful for?

Laughter makes everything feel a little lighter.

Shine Your Light

_____ / _____ / 20_____

What is my word of the day? ________________________________

What HeadTrash do I need to dump from yesterday?

____

____

____

What went well yesterday?

____

____

____

What is important for me to focus on and accomplish today?

____

____

____

At this moment, what am I grateful for?

____

____

____

Negativity only creates more negativity.

#DUMPHeadTrash

_____ / _____ / 20_____

What is my word of the day? ____

What HeadTrash do I need to dump from yesterday?

____

____

____

What went well yesterday?

____

____

____

What is important for me to focus on and accomplish today?

____

____

____

At this moment, what am I grateful for?

____

____

____

I feel the way I think.

Shine Your Light

_____ / _____ / 20_____

What is my word of the day? _______________________________

What HeadTrash do I need to dump from yesterday?

What went well yesterday?

What is important for me to focus on and accomplish today?

At this moment, what am I grateful for?

You have an endless supply of love and get to choose with whom you share it.

#DUMPHeadTrash

_____ / _____ / 20_____

What is my word of the day? _______________________________________

What HeadTrash do I need to dump from yesterday?

What went well yesterday?

What is important for me to focus on and accomplish today?

At this moment, what am I grateful for?

I won't let a bad day make me feel like I have a bad life.

Shine Your Light

_____ / _____ / 20_____

What is my word of the day? ____

What HeadTrash do I need to dump from yesterday?

What went well yesterday?

What is important for me to focus on and accomplish today?

At this moment, what am I grateful for?

The more I give, the more I receive.

#DUMPHeadTrash

____ / ____ / 20___

What is my word of the day? ________________________________

What HeadTrash do I need to dump from yesterday?

What went well yesterday?

What is important for me to focus on and accomplish today?

At this moment, what am I grateful for?

If you are waiting for a sign...this is it!

Shine Your Light

_____ / _____ / 20_____

What is my word of the day? ____

What HeadTrash do I need to dump from yesterday?

What went well yesterday?

What is important for me to focus on and accomplish today?

At this moment, what am I grateful for?

No one can stop me like me!

LOOK INSIDE
a poem by Renie

Look inside, and you will see the beauty
that resides within you.

Your life is a gift to live as you want.

Your inner strength picks you up.

Never, ever quit as who you are is more
than one chapter of your life.

For inside, you have all that you need;
the resilience to persevere,
the ability to captain your
ship through the storms that lie ahead,
and the humility to know
that a new choice is yours to make.

Have faith, look forward, and choose to live a life full
of passion, love, and happiness.

This is your time.

Shine Your Light

_____ / _____ / 20_____

What is my word of the day? ____

What HeadTrash do I need to dump from yesterday?

What went well yesterday?

What is important for me to focus on and accomplish today?

At this moment, what am I grateful for?

The world is not enhanced by negativity, only depleted.

_____ / _____ / 20_____

What is my word of the day? ____

What HeadTrash do I need to dump from yesterday?

____

____

____

What went well yesterday?

____

____

____

What is important for me to focus on and accomplish today?

____

____

____

At this moment, what am I grateful for?

____

____

____

Mindset is the root of all happiness.

Shine Your Light

_____ / _____ / 20 _____

What is my word of the day? ____

What HeadTrash do I need to dump from yesterday?

What went well yesterday?

What is important for me to focus on and accomplish today?

At this moment, what am I grateful for?

You can't pour from an empty cup. Self-care first.

#DUMPHeadTrash

_____ / _____ / 20_____

What is my word of the day? ____

What HeadTrash do I need to dump from yesterday?

____

____

____

What went well yesterday?

____

____

____

What is important for me to focus on and accomplish today?

____

____

____

At this moment, what am I grateful for?

____

____

____

Opportunity is a derivative of adaptability.

Shine Your Light

____ / ____ / 20____

What is my word of the day? _______________________________________

What HeadTrash do I need to dump from yesterday?

What went well yesterday?

What is important for me to focus on and accomplish today?

At this moment, what am I grateful for?

Squash negativity NOW!

_____ / _____ / 20_____

What is my word of the day? ____

What HeadTrash do I need to dump from yesterday?

What went well yesterday?

What is important for me to focus on and accomplish today?

At this moment, what am I grateful for?

Indecision is still a decision. It's just, usually, a bad one.

INSPIRE

a poem by Renie

Who you are

is how you lead

and inspire the world.

When you inspire others,

you help awaken their potential

and as you touch their lives,

they enhance your own.

What is my word of the day? ____

What HeadTrash do I need to dump from yesterday?

____

____

____

What went well yesterday?

____

____

____

What is important for me to focus on and accomplish today?

____

____

____

At this moment, what am I grateful for?

____

____

____

It is easier to get to where I want to go if I have direction.

Shine Your Light

_____ / _____ / 20_____

What is my word of the day? ____

What HeadTrash do I need to dump from yesterday?

What went well yesterday?

What is important for me to focus on and accomplish today?

At this moment, what am I grateful for?

Reflect daily in gratitude. It energizes your soul.

_____ / _____ / 20 _____

What is my word of the day? ____

What HeadTrash do I need to dump from yesterday?

____

____

____

What went well yesterday?

____

____

____

What is important for me to focus on and accomplish today?

____

____

____

At this moment, what am I grateful for?

____

____

____

The more rules I have in my life, the less life I get to live.

Shine Your Light

_____ / _____ / 20 _____

What is my word of the day? ____

What HeadTrash do I need to dump from yesterday?

What went well yesterday?

What is important for me to focus on and accomplish today?

At this moment, what am I grateful for?

Never let anyone convince you that playing small is a good alternative.

#DUMPHeadTrash

_____ / _____ / 20_____

What is my word of the day? ____

What HeadTrash do I need to dump from yesterday?

What went well yesterday?

What is important for me to focus on and accomplish today?

At this moment, what am I grateful for?

For things to change, I must change.

Shine Your Light

_____ / _____ / 20_____

What is my word of the day? ____

What HeadTrash do I need to dump from yesterday?

What went well yesterday?

What is important for me to focus on and accomplish today?

At this moment, what am I grateful for?

My life moves towards what I want through my positive focus and productive actions.

#DUMPHeadTrash

_____ / _____ / 20_____

What is my word of the day? ____

What HeadTrash do I need to dump from yesterday?

What went well yesterday?

What is important for me to focus on and accomplish today?

At this moment, what am I grateful for?

Shine Your Light

_____ / _____ / 20_____

What is my word of the day? ____

What HeadTrash do I need to dump from yesterday?

What went well yesterday?

What is important for me to focus on and accomplish today?

At this moment, what am I grateful for?

Reasonable people adapt to the world, while unreasonable people change it.

THE CHATTERING MIND

a poem by Renie

It is what I cannot hear

that gets in my way.

The noise. So loud.

The chatter. So distracting.

Be still.

Be present.

Let your life unfold and

your potential awaken.

Shine Your Light

____ / ____ / 20___

What is my word of the day? ________________________________

What HeadTrash do I need to dump from yesterday?

What went well yesterday?

What is important for me to focus on and accomplish today?

At this moment, what am I grateful for?

I honor myself by living "ALL IN."

#DUMPHeadTrash

_____ / _____ / 20_____

What is my word of the day? _______________________________

What HeadTrash do I need to dump from yesterday?

What went well yesterday?

What is important for me to focus on and accomplish today?

At this moment, what am I grateful for?

Growth has it's growing pains. Embrace them.

Shine Your Light

_____ / _____ / 20_____

What is my word of the day? ____

What HeadTrash do I need to dump from yesterday?

What went well yesterday?

What is important for me to focus on and accomplish today?

At this moment, what am I grateful for?

Your actions reflect your values.

#DUMPHeadTrash

______ / ______ / 20______

What is my word of the day? ____

What HeadTrash do I need to dump from yesterday?

What went well yesterday?

What is important for me to focus on and accomplish today?

At this moment, what am I grateful for?

A bad attitude is like a flat tire. You can't go anywhere until you change it.

Shine Your Light

_____ / _____ / 20_____

What is my word of the day? ____

What HeadTrash do I need to dump from yesterday?

What went well yesterday?

What is important for me to focus on and accomplish today?

At this moment, what am I grateful for?

Passionate people change the world.

_____ / _____ / 20_____

What is my word of the day? ___________________________________

What HeadTrash do I need to dump from yesterday?

____

____

____

What went well yesterday?

____

____

____

What is important for me to focus on and accomplish today?

____

____

____

At this moment, what am I grateful for?

____

____

____

Laugh more. Criticize less.

Shine Your Light

_____ / _____ / 20 _____

What is my word of the day? _______________________________________

What HeadTrash do I need to dump from yesterday?

What went well yesterday?

What is important for me to focus on and accomplish today?

At this moment, what am I grateful for?

Clarity helps me make courageous choices.

#DUMPHeadTrash

_____ / _____ / 20_____

What is my word of the day? ____

What HeadTrash do I need to dump from yesterday?

What went well yesterday?

What is important for me to focus on and accomplish today?

At this moment, what am I grateful for?

There is nothing as bright as a person who shines from within.

WHAT PEOPLE WANT

a poem by Renie

People want to know you believe in them.
Encourage them.

People want to feel they can trust you.
Talk to them.

People want to learn and grow.
Coach them.

People want to know they are important.
Acknowledge them.

People want to see what is possible.
Give them eyes.

People want to know that their contributions matter.
Recognize them.

People want to feel valued.
Tell them how they are.

People want to feel hope.
Inspire them.

#DUMPHeadTrash

_____ / _____ / 20_____

What is my word of the day? ______________________________

What HeadTrash do I need to dump from yesterday?

What went well yesterday?

What is important for me to focus on and accomplish today?

At this moment, what am I grateful for?

Uncertainty equals opportunity.

Shine Your Light

_____ / _____ / 20 _____

What is my word of the day? ____

What HeadTrash do I need to dump from yesterday?

What went well yesterday?

What is important for me to focus on and accomplish today?

At this moment, what am I grateful for?

Spend your time with people who enhance your life.

#DUMPHeadTrash

____ / ____ / 20____

What is my word of the day? ____

What HeadTrash do I need to dump from yesterday?

What went well yesterday?

What is important for me to focus on and accomplish today?

At this moment, what am I grateful for?

Forward momentum fuels progress.

Shine Your Light

_____ / _____ / 20 _____

What is my word of the day? _______________________________________

What HeadTrash do I need to dump from yesterday?

What went well yesterday?

What is important for me to focus on and accomplish today?

At this moment, what am I grateful for?

Passion makes me dare more, be more, and live more.

FINDING PEACE WITHIN

a poem by Renie

Peace.
That quiet space within.

So hard to find in my ever-chattering mind.
Hard to hear above the loud negative voices
that seem to have taken over.

Peace.
When I sit still and embrace what is right.
When I move from gratitude and respect
my inner truth.

Peace.
When I listen without judgment.
When I embrace my personal power and
let my strength shine through.

Peace.
When my courage steps forward,
and my mind finds stillness.
And then it happens.
The moment of a full breath as I remember
that everything I need is within me.

Peace lives within.

Shine Your Light

_____ / _____ / 20_____

#DUMPHeadTrash

____ / ____ / 20____

Shine Your Light

_____ / _____ / 20_____

#DUMPHeadTrash

_____ / _____ / 20_____

Shine Your Light

_____ / _____ / 20_____

Shine Your Light

____ / ____ / 20____

Shine Your Light

_____ / _____ / 20_____

#DUMPHeadTrash

_____ / _____ / 20_____

Shine Your Light

____ / ____ / 20____

_____ / _____ / 20_____

Shine Your Light

____ / ____ / 20____

#DUMPHeadTrash

_____ / _____ / 20_____

Shine Your Light

_____ / _____ / 20_____

#DUMPHeadTrash

_____ / _____ / 20_____

Shine Your Light

____ / ____ / 20____

_____ / _____ / 20_____

Shine Your Light

____ / ____ / 20____

#DUMPHeadTrash

_____ / _____ / 20_____

Shine Your Light

___ / ___ / 20___

#DUMPHeadTrash

___ / ___ / 20___

Shine Your Light

_____ / _____ / 20_____

#DUMPHeadTrash

_____ / _____ / 20_____

9 781792 353291